Pirate Treasure

Written by Maribeth Boelts

Illustrated by Rob Mancini

The pirates pack their trunk.

"Pirate hats?" says Red.

"Check," says Sam.

"Parrot seed?" says Red.

"Check," says Pete.

"Treasure map?" says Red.

The pirates look all around.
There is no map.

"We don't need a map," says Sam.

The pirates sail away to look for treasure.

They drop their net and catch a shoe.

They drop their net again.
They catch a bucket.

They drop their net again.
They catch something big.

It's Red!

"Can't a pirate take a bath?"
says Red.

8

The pirates start to cry.

"We'll never find the treasure!" they say.

Salty, the parrot, flies by.
There is something in his beak.

"It's the map!" says Sam.

"Follow that parrot!" says Pete.

The pirates follow the parrot.

Soon he drops the map,
and the pirates read it.

"This is the place!" says Red.

The pirates drop their net.

They do not catch a shoe or a bucket.
They do not catch a pirate.

They catch a TREASURE!

"Hurray!" shout the pirates.

15

"Squawk!" says Salty.